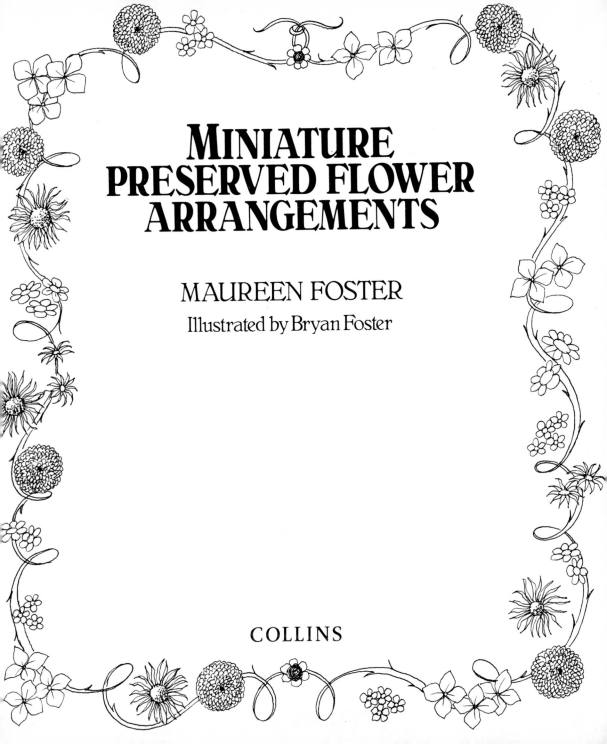

MINIATURE PRESERVED FLOWER ARRANGEMENTS

MAUREEN FOSTER

Illustrated by Bryan Foster

COLLINS

Plate 1 *Gold flowers in perfect harmony*
with a brass candlestick

First published in 1985
by William Collins Sons & Co. Ltd
London . Glasgow . Sydney
Auckland . Toronto . Johannesburg

ISBN 0 00 411605 4

Set in Linotron Souvenir
by Rowland Phototypesetting Ltd
Printed and bound in Italy
by New Interlitho, Milan

CONTENTS

Introduction 9
**1 Plant Materials
and How to Preserve Them** 10
Flowers 10
Foliage 18
Seeds, seedheads and seed capsules 20
Grasses 22
Cones 23
Mosses and lichens 23

2 Arrangements 24
Containers 24
Making archways 38
Bases 39
Creating miniature landscapes 40
Displaying miniature arrangements 44

**3 Plaques, Pictures
and Victorian Novelties** 46
Plaques 48
Miniature posy 52
Flower arrangement greetings card 54
Parasol 56
Decorated fan 58

INTRODUCTION

For anyone like myself who enjoys and is fascinated by tiny things, creating miniature arrangements with preserved plant materials can open up a whole new and exciting world. I can think of few more enjoyable and inexpensive hobbies which can be practised throughout the year. Readers of my book *The Art of Preserved Flower Arrangement* will be aware of the difficulty I experienced when trying to cover the subject of miniature arrangements in only one chapter. It was at that time that the idea of a whole book on miniatures was born.

The possibilities of miniature flower arranging are endless because the limitations, namely time and the ability to look and observe plant materials which are of the correct scale, are self-orientated. Plant materials can of course be gathered during all the seasons of the year and, if carefully stored, this makes it easy for readers without

Plate 2 *A discarded egg timer makes an unusual container for an arrangement*

gardens to collect whenever the occasion arises, either from a friend's garden or the countryside. Another attractive feature of preserved miniatures is that because of their size, plant materials, containers and accessories need little storage or working space.

My love for fresh flowers has always remained somewhat reserved when it comes to miniature arrangements. It is tantalizing to be rewarded by their beauty for such a relatively short time and this, for me, limits this aspect of flower arranging to simple arrangements of 'in season' treasures from my garden. The more intricate designs are best created with preserved plant materials.

I always welcome tiny paper bags of unusual bits and pieces from friends who think of me while holidaying abroad, and many of these hoarded treasures can be found in my arrangements where they serve as constant reminders of those who provided them. Maybe they too are looking at the countryside through fresh eyes and seeing beauty in unusual seedpods or dried flower skeletons.

PLANT MATERIALS AND HOW TO PRESERVE THEM

A flower arranger working with preserved plant materials has distinct advantages over the arranger of fresh flowers. The ability to create an arrangement at any time of the year, incorporating preserved plant materials from different seasons, allows the arranger to plan colour schemes in advance. Creating an arrangement without the need for water means that, if necessary, stems can be wired, not only to increase their length but also to enable them to be bent at various angles. This can often help to accentuate a particular line or style. The plant materials used for the illustrations in this book are shown in Plates 3 and 4.

FLOWERS

In the majority of arrangements, both large and small, it is the flowers which provide most of the colour. When preserved flowers are used it is important that these should retain their natural colour and form to avoid the dried and lifeless look which in the past was so often attributed to these arrangements. To do this effectively it is necessary to extract the flower's natural moisture completely, while keeping its shape and form. Apart from those mentioned in the section on natural preserving (page 14), all flowers can only be successfully preserved in a desiccant. This method is described on page 15.

Unless a large rock garden is readily available or the arranger has access to miniature plants, the range of larger plants and shrubs from which snippets of flowering spikes or sprays can be gathered is limited. There are, however, many flowers which consist of one or more clusters of individual florets, which can be cut away from the main stem and preserved complete with their own tiny portion of stem. These provide ideal material for pictures and plaques (see Fig. 1). Stems can easily be lengthened if necessary: just glue a length of florists' silver wire to the side of the flower's natural stem as shown in Fig. 3a

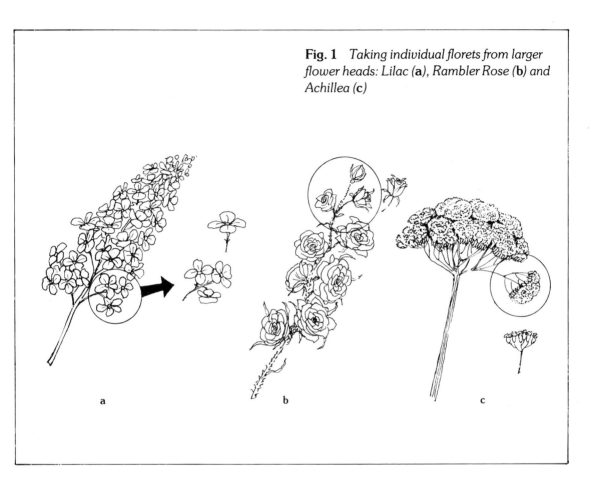

Fig. 1 *Taking individual florets from larger flower heads: Lilac (**a**), Rambler Rose (**b**) and Achillea (**c**)*

a

b

c

(page 15). These wire stems can then be concealed in an arrangement by the other plant materials. Miniature flowering spikes can also be made by gluing several florets to individual wires (see Fig. 3b, page 15). Flowers which can be successfully cut up and used in this way include Lilac, Rambler Roses, Achillea (see Fig. 1), Delphinium, Deutzia, Feverfew, Hydrangea, Montbretia, Philadelphus (mock orange blossom), Solomon's Seal, Statice and Spiraea Arguta.

CALYCES

The calyces of certain flowers provide interesting flower-like shapes, and although many of them are too large for miniatures, some suitable ones can be found. Ballota, much loved by flower arrangers for its curious twisting stems of tiny green woolly calyces, is an ideal example; each calyx can be cut away from the main stem and used in the same way as individual florets (Fig. 1).

Plate 3 *Flowers and buds used in the arrangements*

1 *Rosa* (Rose 'Dorothy Perkins')
2 *Fuchsia* – small single-flowered varieties
3 *Centaurea cyanus* (Cornflower)
4 *Rosa* (Miniature Rose 'Meirov')
5 *Saxifraga* (Mossy Saxifrage)
6 *Ageratum*
7 *Auricula*
8 *Limonium* (Statice)
9 *Erica* (Heather)
10 *Prunus serrulata* (Flowering Cherry)
11 *Rosa* (Rose)
12 *Crataegus monogyna* (Common Hawthorn or May)
13 *Syringa* (Lilac)
14 *Centaurea cyanus* (Cornflower)
15 *Hydrangea* – Hortensia varieties
16 *Hyacinthus* (Hyacinth)
17 *Helichrysum* (Strawflower)
18 *Astilbe* (False Goat's Beard)
19 *Rosa* (Rose 'Cécile Brunner')
20 *Limonium vulgara* (Sea Lavender)
21 *Myosotis* (Forget-me-not)
22 *Delphinium* – small single-flowered varieties
23 *Lavandula* (Lavender)
24 *Sedum*
25 *Chrysanthemum*
26 *Hydrangea* – Lace-cap varieties
27 *Bellis perennis* (Daisy)
28 *Hosta fortunei* (Plantain Lily)
29 *Gypsophila paniculata* (Baby's Breath)
30 *Spiraea arguta*
31 *Alchemilla* (Lady's Mantle)
32 *Ornithogalum nutans*
33 *Allium schoenoprasum* (Chives)
34 *Tagetes patula* (French Marigold)
35 *Dianthus* – Florists' spray carnation
36 *Xeranthemum*
37 *Limonium latifolium* (Sea Lavender)
38 *Ornithogalum thyrsoides*
39 *Ballota pseudodictamnus*
40 *Achillea clypeolata* (Yarrow)
41 *Viburnum rhytidophyllum*
42 *Campanula Allionii Rubra* (Bell Flower)
43 *Glitzia*
44 *Saxifraga* (Mossy Saxifrage)
45 *Chrysanthemum parthenium* (Feverfew)
46 *Sambucus nigra* (Elder)
47 *Deutzia*
48 *Polygonatum multiflorum* (Solomon's Seal)
49 *Chrysanthemum*
50 *Anthemis tinctoria* (Ox-eye Chamomile)
51 *Crocosmiiflora* (Montbretia)
52 *Potentilla fruticosa* ('Tangerine')
53 *Tagetes patula* (French Marigold)
54 *Lonas* (African Daisy)
55 *Helichrysum* (Strawflower)
56 *Kerria japonica 'Flore pleno'* (Jew's Mallow)
57 *Philadelphus* (Mock Orange)
58 *Ranunculus ficaria* (Lesser Celandine)
59 *Ammobium alatum*
60 *Helipterum* (Winged Everlasting)
61 *Limonium* (Statice)
62 *Tagetes patula* (French Marigold)
63 *Rudbeckia sullivantii* (Cone Flower)
64 *Santolina chamaecyparissus* (Lavender Cotton)

FLOWERS WHICH DRY NATURALLY

Owing to their papery texture, the groups of flowers known as everlastings or strawflowers will dry to perfection without any special treatment. Just hang them in small bunches in a warm, dark and airy place until the stems are dry and firm enough to support the flower heads. Helichrysums are the most widely known of the everlastings, although for miniatures it will only be possible to use the tiny flowers which form on the side of the main flower stem. The annual Statice is useful if used as illustrated in Fig. 1, and you will also find Helipterum and the smaller flowers of Xeranthemum and Acroclinium are particularly attractive. The size, formation and density of their petals enable a few other flowers, such as Achillea, Lavender and Heather, to respond successfully to this simple method of preservation.

PRESERVING FLOWERS IN DESICCANTS

A desiccant is a substance which absorbs moisture. Sand, alum, cornmeal, starch and detergent powders all act as desiccants, but while these are worth experimenting with, readers should be aware that only varying degrees of success can be expected from them. A desiccant needs to be quick-acting, and I find these are not. Household borax is an effective desiccant, however, providing it is used dry and free from lumps, and it is ideal for most tiny flowers. The disadvantages of this method are that a warm airing cupboard is necessary to complete the pre-

Fig. 2 *Flower positioning for desiccant preserving*

serving process, and a powdery residue is often found clinging to the petals after preserving, which must be brushed off with an artist's painting brush.

Silica gel crystals, together with silica gel-based products, make the most efficient desiccants. Providing these are of a fine, even grade they are suitable for all types of flowers, both large and small. All are sold complete with reactivating instructions, which means that they are reusable over an infinite period. It is also possible to obtain these products in powder form, but I find that like borax this is inclined to cling.

Plate 3 shows a selection of the flowers which I have used for the arrangements in this book; these can be used as a guide to the most suitable types of flowers to choose for preserving by this method. Make sure that you gather the flowers when they are dry.

METHOD FOR DESICCANT PRESERVING

It is important to use the correct container: cardboard boxes without lids for borax and other similar desiccants; and tins with airtight lids for silica gel-based products. Spoon the desiccant into the bottom of the appropriate type of container to form a layer approximately 12 mm (½ in) deep. Position the flowers in rows so that it is easy to cover them with the desiccant; Fig. 2 illustrates the most successful positioning for different flower shapes. Carefully spoon the desiccant in between the rows of flowers, allowing the crystals or powder to fall naturally in between and over the petals. Never attempt to spoon the desiccant directly on top of the flowers, with the exception of borax which may be sieved. When the flowers are completely covered, mark your container with the date and its contents. An open box of flowers in borax should be placed in a warm airing cupboard, while an airtight tin of flowers in silica gel can be kept in any safe place.

The time needed to complete the preserving process will vary according to the density of the petals, but it is usually a minimum of two days and a maximum of ten. Ideally each batch should be restricted to one type of flower but this is not always practical when tiny flowers are preserved, so I would suggest the maximum time is allowed for boxes of mixed flowers. To remove the flowers, carefully pour off the desiccant by letting it fall slowly through your fingers. This will enable you to catch the flowers with the minimum of damage. Tiny flowers will be very brittle at this stage and require careful

Fig. 3 *Lengthening a flower stem (**a**) and making a flower spike (**b**)*

handling. It is inevitable that a small percentage will get broken and have to be discarded. If, after preserving, it is necessary to strengthen the flower stems, I find the easiest way to do this is to glue a length of florists' silver wire to the side of the stem, as shown in Fig. 3a.

STORING DESICCANT-PRESERVED FLOWERS

Experience has taught me that it is most satisfactory to store tiny flowers in colour groups. Small coffee tins or shallow biscuit tins are ideal for this, providing the tin is airtight. It is important to cover the bottom of the tin with a layer of *dry* desiccant, which will absorb any moisture which may remain hidden in either the flowers or the tin.

Plate 4 *Leaves, seedheads and calyces used in the arrangements*

1 *Chamaecyparis lawsoniana 'Lutea'* (Lawson's Cypress)
2 *Acer rubrum* (Maple)
3 *Dianthus* (Rock Garden Pinks)
4 *Salvia officinalis 'Purpurea'* (Common Sage)
5 *Cyclamen neapolitanum*
6 *Hebi 'Pagei'*
7 *Asplenium trichomanes* (Maidenhair Spleenwort)
8 *Tellima*
9 *Viburnum rhytidophyllum*
10 *Acaena*
11 *Eucalyptus gunnii* (Gum Tree) – young foliage
12 *Buxus Sempervirens* (Common Box)
13 *Rhus cotinus* (Smoke Bush)
14 *Ranunculus ficaria* (Lesser Celandine)
15 *Crataegus monogyna* (Common Hawthorn or May)
16 *Clematis montana*
17 *Vitis henryana* (Vine)
18 *Salvia officinalis 'Tricolor'* (Common Sage)
19 *Salvia officinalis 'Icterina'* (Common Sage)
20 *Ruta 'Jackmans' Blue'* (Rue)
21 *Senecio cineraria*
22 *Choisya* (Mexican Orange Blossom)
23 *Santolina chamaecyparissus* (Lavender Cotton)
24 *Viburnum opulus* (Guelder Rose)
25 *Artemisia* (Wormwood)
26 *Cotoneaster franchetii*
27 *Stachys lanata*
28 *Ajuga reptans 'Atropurpurea'*
29 *Plantago media* (Plantain)
30 *Hedera* (Ivy) – small-leaf varieties
31 *Clematis Etoile Violette*
32 *Chrysanthemum haradjanii*
33 *Elaeagnus pungens 'Macrophylla'*
34 *Crocosmiiflora* (Montbretia)
35 *Mediterranean seedhead*
36 *Acaena*
37 *Ruta 'Jackmans' Blue'* (Rue)
38 *Papaver rhoeas* (Common Red Poppy)
39 *Doronicum* (Leopard's Bane)

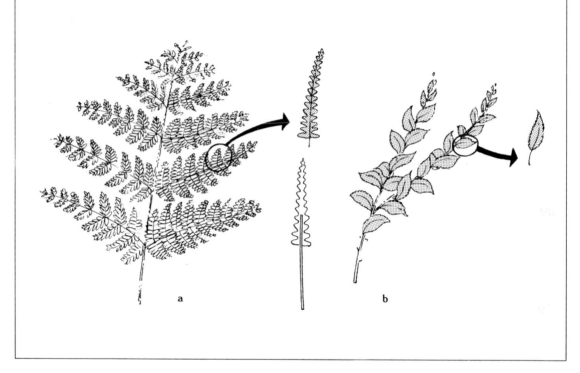

Fig. 4 *Making individual ferns from a bracken frond (**a**) and using small individual leaves from a leafy branch (**b**)*

a

b

FOLIAGE

Leaves for miniature arrangements, plaques and pictures must obviously be small and in proportion with the flowers. Many alpine and herbaceous plants will provide suitable leaves in a wide range of colours and these can be successfully preserved by the desiccant method described for flowers on page 15. It is important, however, to select leaves with a firm texture, for many of them will tend to be rather brittle when preserved and need careful handling. My favourite miniature foliage is without doubt the tiny evergreen ferns of the Maidenhair Spleenwort, found growing on the crumbling mortar of old walls; these are absolutely perfect for all types of miniatures. As these ferns are not always easy to find, the common bracken fern provides a good substitute. The formation of each frond enables the arranger to cut away segments of different sizes from the main stem. A length of florists' wire can then

18

be glued to the back of the central rib of each segment, providing a collection of miniature ferns ready for use (see Fig. 4a).

Many trees and shrubs have tiny leaves and, when fully mature, small woody branches of these leaves can be gathered and preserved by the glycerine method described below. After preserving, each leaf can be cut away as shown in Fig. 4b. It will be necessary to attach false stems to the leaves as shown for ferns (see Fig. 4a). Although most foliage for miniatures is preserved by the desiccant or glycerine method, one exception is the foliage from the many evergreen cypress trees which will dry naturally because of the leaf formation and firm structure. Just cut the leaves and lay them in a dry, dark place.

Remembering that miniatures are of course only scaled-down replicas of larger arrangements, it is of equal importance to consider the colour of the foliage and its relationship with the flowers. To enable harmonious effects to be created between flowers and foliage, reference to Plate 4 will be helpful when foliage is selected for use in a particular colour scheme. Obviously there is not always a definite dividing line between each colour and therefore certain variations in colour are inevitable.

Fig. 5 *Mixing a suitable glycerine solution for preserving*

METHOD FOR GLYCERINE PRESERVING

Use a rust-proof container which is just large enough to hold your foliage comfortably without fear of it becoming squashed. Small mustard or pickle jars are ideal. Add one part of glycerine to two parts of hot water (see Fig. 5) and mix together well until the mixture is clear. Glycerine is heavier than water and unless you mix thoroughly the glycerine will remain at the bottom and only the water will be taken up by the foliage.

A depth of about 76 mm (3 in) of the mixture will usually be necessary. For support, stand the container inside another container which is large enough to prevent the foliage toppling over. Recut and split the stem of the foliage and put it into the hot mixture. Leave your container of foliage to

19

stand in a dry, airy place, away from direct light and in a warm atmosphere. Thin, textured leaves will take about four days to preserve, while thicker leaves may take two weeks or even more. Some leaves will change colour and I particularly like leaves such as Escallonia which turn almost black. It is important to remove the leaves before they become saturated with the mixture, and care must be taken to dry the stems.

I find the following groups of plant materials particularly fascinating as I continue to appreciate the beauty of nature's less obvious gems of the plant world. But be warned: owing to their subdued colouring it often requires a keen and well-trained eye to locate them in their natural habitat. The decorative value of all these plant materials lies mainly in their shape and form. The selection that I have chosen to illustrate will, I hope, guide the arranger in the search for plant materials which will give an arrangement extra interest.

Fig. 6 *Seedheads drying naturally*

SEEDS, SEEDHEADS AND SEED CAPSULES

Round, flat, spiky and pendula are all terms used to describe this group of plant materials. It is with these materials in mind that I have chosen the selection in Plate 4, which are no more than a representation of different shapes and forms. I hope these will help readers to develop an awareness of the seeds, seedheads or individual seed capsules which are to be found in their own gardens, however small, or in the countryside around them. Remember that even in towns, waste ground and old crumbling walls are valuable areas to explore, for often the most interesting seedheads develop on the most common of plants.

Most seedheads will eventually dry naturally on the plant but by then, although ready for immediate use, most will have been bleached by the sun and rain and will be valuable mainly for their shape and form. To capture more interesting and colourful seedheads, pick them as soon as they are fully developed and firm, and stand them in tiny pots, such as paste pots (see Fig. 6), allowing them to dry off naturally, but away from direct light.

Plate 5 *Interesting containers: duck eggshell (A), dish (B), bottle (C) and piece of slate (D)*

A

B

C

D

21

Fig. 7 *Making a 'fun flower'*

Fig. 8 *A selection of wild grasses illustrating a wide variation of forms*

MAKING FUN FLOWERS

Readers of my book *The Art of Preserved Flower Arrangement* will be familiar with the term 'fun flowers' as one that I use to describe flowers made up from a range of plant parts. This idea can also be used in connection with preserved miniature arrangements, providing the plant parts are small enough in scale and the structure is kept relatively simple; Fig. 7 illustrates a good example. Almost any tiny seedhead complete with its own stem will provide a flower centre around which to glue leaf 'petals'. Small leaves taken from sprays of glycerined Box or Escallonia are ideal plant shapes to use. The number necessary for each flower will depend on the size of whatever you choose to use for a centre. Little desiccant-preserved autumn leaves also make attractive flowers; in Plate 2 I used *Cotoneaster Horizontalis*.

GRASSES

Many of the smaller species of grasses, wild and cultivated (see Fig. 8), add grace and charm to a miniature arrangement of flowers; but to appreciate their beauty more fully I also like to arrange them with tiny seedheads, for their delicate forms and subtle green and mauve colourings are not overpowered by the more brilliant colouring of flowers. An example of such an arrangement is shown in Plate 7A. Gather wild grasses from May to June; cultivated grasses should be gathered as the flower heads form. Grasses are preserved like seedheads (page 20).

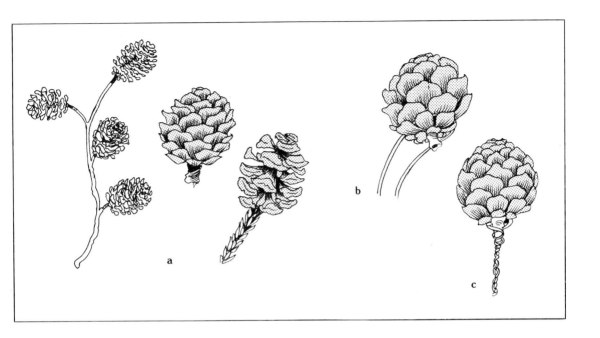

CONES

Fig. 9 *A selection of suitable cones for miniature arrangements (a) and how to wire a cone (b and c)*

Much as I love cones for their flower-like shapes or intriguing, intricate forms, very few are small enough to use in miniature work. Those that are, namely Alder, Japanese Larch and the Wellingtonia Cypress, can be seen in Fig. 9a. These are truly delightful and can be used in miniature plaques, pictures or arrangements. They will of course need to be wired for arrangements. Using a fine-gauge florists' wire, bend the wire in half and thread it between the bottom two rows of cone scales (see Fig. 9b). When you pull the wire taut it will become embedded between the cone scales. Twist the two ends of the wire together and wind them round the little nodule of stem (see Fig. 9c).

MOSSES AND LICHENS

Emerald green mosses can be gathered at almost any time, but periods of drought should be avoided, for at such times mosses may appear brown, dull and shrivelled. All moss will dry naturally if kept away from direct light. Moss is ideal to use as the basis for a typical meadow landscape design, as illustrated in Plate 11A. In contrast, lichen, which also dries naturally and requires no special treatment, can be effectively used when creating a mountainous landscape (see Plate 11D).

ARRANGEMENTS

The requirements for miniature flower arranging are very simple. You will need either a container or a base in or on which to make your arrangement. Sometimes you will need both as certain types of containers are made in such a way that to stand them on a base helps to balance the completed arrangement visually. Within an arrangement figurines, used either as an integral part of the container or as accessories, can add interest and create a sense of movement. Animals, too, can be used and can inspire the arranger to create tiny realistic scenes. My own collection of different containers, accessories and bases, and the way in which I have used them, will, I hope, help and encourage the novice and inspire the experienced flower arranger. Maybe you will also discover, as I have, that collecting these items can be an equally absorbing and exciting part of miniature flower arranging as collecting and preserving the plant materials themselves.

CONTAINERS

Ideal containers are not necessarily those which at first appear to be an obvious choice. I get far more fun and enjoyment from using items other than the more usual jug, pot or traditional flower container. This book features a wide selection of my own containers, some of which are unusual but most of which are readily available. With a quick glance around their own homes, most arrangers will be able to find something to use as a miniature container. Local junk shops, market stalls or bring-and-buy sales are also useful sources to explore: boxes marked 'TO CLEAR' can be particularly rewarding. To the untrained eye, the contents of these may appear to be nothing more than useless junk, but once some experience has been gained in working with miniatures,

Plate 6 *Flowerless arrangement* (A), *clam shell arrangement* (B), *and miniature table setting* (C)

A

B

C

25

Fig. 10 *Making a miniature candle holder from a beech nut husk (**a**) and a miniature container from a poppy seedcase (**b** and **c**)*

the eye of a flower arranger automatically sees the potential in all kinds of bits and pieces. I have proved the saying 'One man's trash is another man's treasure' to be true on many occasions. In fact, the egg timer stand with its missing glass illustrated in Plate 2 was given to me by an antique-stall holder who exclaimed, 'Oh, that! You are more than welcome to take it; it's no use to anyone without its glass.' Because I could appreciate its interesting shape I immediately thought of it in connection with preserved flowers. I found it was necessary to leave it in a prominent position for a few days until I could eventually decide how best to relate it to a style of arrangement. Having decided this, it

was relatively easy to select suitable plant materials of the appropriate scale.

NATURE AS DESIGNER

During many years of working with preserved plant materials I have learned to appreciate the remarkable shapes and forms not only of flowers but of the many less obvious plant parts such as grasses, leaves and seedheads. My book *Creating Patterns with Grasses, Leaves, Seedheads and Cones* was a direct result of this, and while working on the book I became infinitely more aware of the structure of seedcases, often visualizing them as beautifully constructed minia-

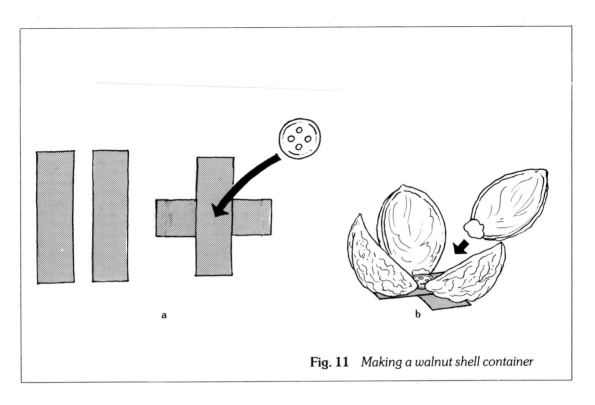

a

b

Fig. 11 *Making a walnut shell container*

ture containers, or as parts from which to make a unique container. For this reason I am including here several examples of my ideas for using seedcases in this way. Once you begin to look at seedcases you will discover many more. Really tiny ones – for example, a poppy seedcase – make perfect containers in which to create miniature arrangements for dolls' houses, and with this in mind I made a simple table with a flower-decorated cloth on which to display an arrangement in a poppy seedhead container (see Plate 6c). To complete the table setting I made two miniature candle holders from beech nut husks, using the tops of poppy seedcases for bases (see Fig. 10a). The table

is made from cardboard cut in an oval shape with a cotton reel stuck at each end.

Making a poppy seedcase into a container
Using a sharp craft knife, cut off about one third of the stem end of a poppy seedcase (see Fig. 10b). The top of the seedcase now becomes the base of the container. Sand, tiny pebbles or even gravel used to fill about two thirds of the container will add weight and ensure against it toppling over. A piece of flower foam is then pushed into the top of the opening to take the plant materials as shown in Fig. 10c. Let it protrude about 6 mm (¼ in) above the container to allow stems to be inserted at an angle.

Fig. 12 *Fixing two halves of a cockle shell together to make a container*

Fig. 13 *Using a shell as an accessory in an arrangement*

Making a walnut shell container

An interesting and unusual container can be made using empty walnut shells. Cut two pieces of thin cardboard 32 × 6 mm (1¼ × ¼ in). Glue these together at right angles to form a cross, and in the centre glue a small shirt button (see Fig. 11a). Apply a blob of glue to one end of each shell and position them as in Fig. 11b. To ensure the cluster of shells remains at the desired angle, hold it with your hands, or some other form of support, for a few minutes until the glue is sufficiently set to hold it in place. A small lump of plasticine or floral clay pressed on to the button will provide sufficient anchorage for the stems of your plant materials.

Seashells

There are, of course, many natural objects other than seedcases which can be used as interesting containers for miniature arrangements. I find seashells particularly fascinating as I feel they have an affinity with plant materials. Some are free-standing but it will often be necessary to fix two shells together with a small blob of quick-drying glue, providing the shell which forms the base will stand firmly and evenly. The two shells need not be identical. Fig. 12a shows how two halves of a cockle shell can be stuck together as nature designed them, but supported in an open position with the aid of two small pieces of rigid cardboard glued in position as shown. A curtain ring glued to the underneath of the base shell enables the container to stand firmly, as shown in Fig. 12b.

Plate 7 *Seashells harmonize with a variety of plant materials*

A

B

C

D

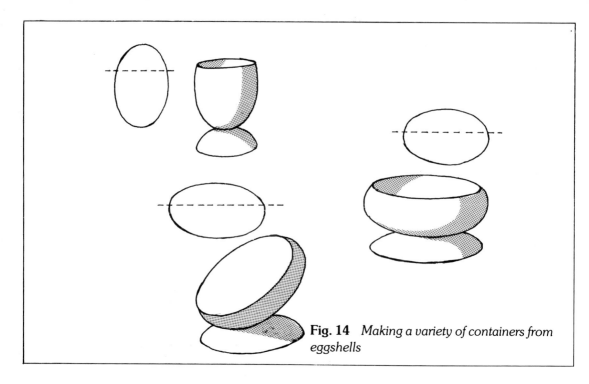

Fig. 14 *Making a variety of containers from eggshells*

Some shells should be considered for use as accessories within an arrangement, particularly if they have interesting markings or beautiful iridescent colourings. To use such shells as containers would conceal rather than enhance these qualities. Fig. 13 illustrates how to use a shell in this way, simply by positioning and pressing it into a lump of self-hardening modelling clay or plasticine on a suitable base. Sufficient modelling clay should be allowed in which to arrange the plant materials.

Eggshells

The eggshell is yet another type of natural shell from which an interesting container can be made. In recent years the art of decorat-

ing eggs has become a much practised craft, involving the use of many special accessories such as hinges, braids and stands. In this book I have used the eggshell in its natural state to make simple containers for preserved flowers. Choose from white or brown hen or pullet eggs, depending on the size of container required and the choice of colour scheme for the arrangement. For a special container search for a duck egg; its beautiful delicate colourings can vary from shades of bluey green to greeny blue.

Eggs can be cut in half length- or widthways, using either a small, fine-toothed hacksaw or even a serrated kitchen knife. Fig. 14 shows how to make differently shaped containers simply by varying the

Fig. 15 *Supporting the lid of a box in a half-open position*

antique can be safely used. Regardless of value, boxes both plain and decorative come in a wide range of shapes and are made from a variety of materials, the colour of which can be an indication as to the type and colouring of plant materials to choose. Boxes generally offer very little scope for variation in style of arrangement, which is usually casual and unsophisticated, as plant materials appear to spill out from under their propped-open lids. To support half-open lids in this way, cut a piece of florists' foam to fit the box, allowing it to come slightly above the rim (see Fig. 15), and either wedge it directly into the box or first wrap it in tissue paper to protect the inside of your box. Prop the lid open at the required angle with two halves of a matchstick inserted into the foam as shown.

angle at which the two eggshells are stuck together. Having decided on the desired angle, a blob of quick-drying contact adhesive at the point where the two halves touch will ensure a secure bond, although it will be necessary to hold them in place for a few minutes until the glue is dry. An alternative and less permanent method of fixing can be achieved by using a small knob of florists' fixative.

BOXES

Miniature boxes, whether new or antique, make perfect containers for preserved miniature arrangements. As the need for water is obviated, even the most treasured

BASKETS

Whatever the current style or fashion in flower arrangement containers, baskets remain very much favoured by flower arrangers, particularly for casual arrangements of garden flowers. Scaled-down miniature baskets made from cane are usually easy to find in florists' or rural craft shops. Attractive imported metal ones are also available from time to time, and as a result of the vogue in past years for plastic flowers, miniature plastic baskets filled with these rather crude imitations can often be found on charity stalls, at jumble sales or in junk shops. Discard the plastic flowers and you are left with a delightful little basket. In Plate 15A you can see one of these baskets, which I sprayed with gold paint.

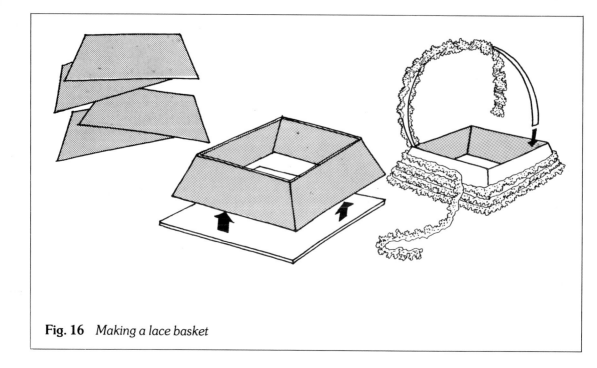

Fig. 16 *Making a lace basket*

Lace basket

You might like to copy my idea of making a typically Victorian basket in which dainty preserved flowers can be arranged. You will need: stiff cardboard, thin pliable card, approximately 1.83 m (2 yds) of 12 mm (½ in) wide lace, and some contact glue. Cut four pieces of stiff cardboard, each one measuring 44 mm (1¾ in) along the bottom, 32 mm (1¼ in) along the top, and 18 mm (¾ in) wide. Stick the four pieces together to form the sides of the basket as shown in Fig. 16. Cut a 44 mm (1¾ in) square of cardboard and glue this in place to form the bottom of the basket. Leaving aside about 305 mm (12 in) of lace for the handle, gather along one edge of the remaining length of

lace. It is not necessary to gather the lace very tightly but it is important to use very small stitches. Glue the gathered edge of the lace round the cardboard shape to form five rows (see Fig. 16). Gather the remaining piece of lace with a central row of gathering stitches. Cut a strip of thin card 6 × 254 mm (¼ × 10 in) for the handle. Cover one side of the card with glue and attach the lace, then glue the ends of the handle to the inside corners of the basket. A small block of floral foam can be securely fixed to the inside of the basket with a blob of glue.

Plate 8 *Lace basket (A), and arrangements using a dolls' house table (B), plate (C) and mirror (D)*

A

B

C

D

PLATES, SAUCERS AND DISHES

Plates, saucers and dishes, whether old or new, make good containers for miniature arrangements. Those from a doll's service are an obvious choice, but it is also possible to find small brass and silver ones, or at least their imitations. If you cannot find any suitable plates or dishes, however, try using tiny plant pot saucers; these are readily available from garden centres or stockists of garden sundries, and the cost is within everyone's budget. Fig. 17 shows how a lump of plasticine was pressed into position to take an arrangement. Decorated plates and saucers can be effectively used as accessories as well; their colour can be the inspiration for the choice of plant materials, as Plate 8c illustrates.

Fig. 17 *Plasticine being used to hold the stems of plant materials*

CANDLESTICKS

Miniature candlesticks are relatively easy to find, particularly inexpensive reproduction brass ones. To use them as containers is not so easy, however, as even the smallest candlecup holder that can be bought from a florist is only suitable for use in a full-size candlestick. For this reason I have always made my own holders from a bottle or jar top and a cork. This is very simple to do, and of course each one can be tailor-made to fit any size candlestick. First, find a suitable-size bottle top and a small cork. The cork should be just the right size to fit firmly and securely into the top of the candlestick; if it is too large, shave down one end with a sharp knife. Apply glue to the other end of the cork and attach it to the outside of the bottle top (see Fig. 18). Leave overnight to ensure a strong adhesion. Cut a piece of flower foam about twice the depth of the holder and wedge it firmly in place. The added depth will enable you to insert some plant materials at an angle to create a downward flow in the arrangement (see Plate 1). Finally, fix the holder in the top of your candlestick so that it is ready to use.

BOTTLES

Throwaway items such as miniature bottles can be adapted to make interesting containers. I am quite sure that even readers without any previous interest in flower arranging will have some empty miniature liqueur or perfume bottles tucked away, for no other

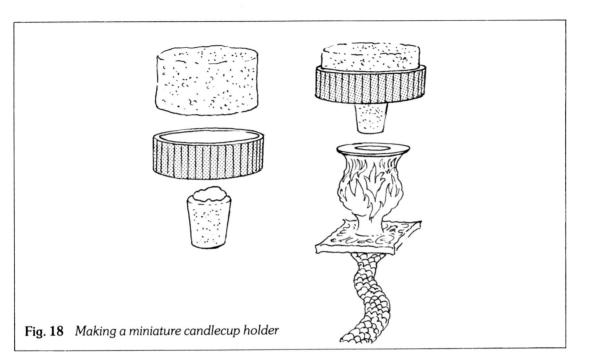

Fig. 18 *Making a miniature candlecup holder*

reason than that they are just too attractive to throw away. Many such bottles are made from coloured glass and will provide the basic colour around which your arrangement can be planned. Bottles made from clear glass can be made to look more attractive when filled with diluted food colouring. A holder which will fit into the neck of the bottle is made in the same way as the one described for candlesticks (see above), using the bottle's own cork if it has one. Bottle tops can also be used as miniature containers.

JUGS

Gift shops at home and abroad are probably the most likely places in which to find new miniature jugs. Alternatively, scour junk shops for worthless old ones or antique shops if the budget permits. A young daughter may even be persuaded to lend one from her doll's tea service. Once you have chosen your jug, regardless of size, wedge a piece of florists' foam into the neck to take your arrangement. Alternatively, plasticine or floral clay can be used.

PEDESTALS

Full-size flower arrangements are often made on pedestals, but this is not so simple with miniatures. The reason for this is that miniature pedestals for flower arranging are not readily available; but as so often happens when I find myself in the position of wanting something which is not available,

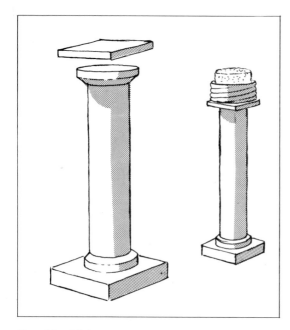

Fig. 19 *Making a miniature pedestal from a plastic cotton reel*

the solution to the problem is to make one. After much thought as to how this should be done, I discovered that a plastic cotton reel makes an ideal pillar on which to stick cardboard shapes which form the top and base of the pedestal (see Fig. 19). The size of these shapes should of course be in proportion to the size of the cotton reel, and as these vary so much I will not attempt to give measurements here. When the pedestal is complete, find a suitable-size bottle top and stick this on to take the arrangement. Fix the floral foam as shown in Fig. 18.

An inexpensive pedestal-type container can also be made by using a tiny plant pot saucer as described on page 34. Choose a bottle top of a suitable size and shape, and

stick it to the underside of the saucer. Refer to Fig. 18 for fixing the floral foam. The completed container can then be painted to suit any chosen colour scheme.

FIGURINES AS CONTAINERS

Figurines in the form of containers are not easy to find but they are well worth searching for. It is very rewarding when you find something which is absolutely ideal. The graceful figurine in Plate 9B is a modern Italian import, although its delicate, subdued colouring and beautiful features give it the appearance of being an antique. The little container incorporating a cherub in Plate 9C is an antique, however, and one I just could not resist buying. The opening of the actual container (less than 12 mm/½ in across) makes it unsuitable for a fresh flower arrangement because it would take only about four stems. With placements of floral clay pressed firmly in position both in and on the container, it is relatively easy to create an appropriate arrangement with preserved plant materials. Although it is unlikely that the reader will have an identical container, I hope that the way in which I have used this one may provide inspiration for using a similar difficult container which would not normally be considered suitable for a flower arrangement.

Plate 9 *Cotton reel pedestal, and figurines used as containers and accessories*

36

A

B

C

D

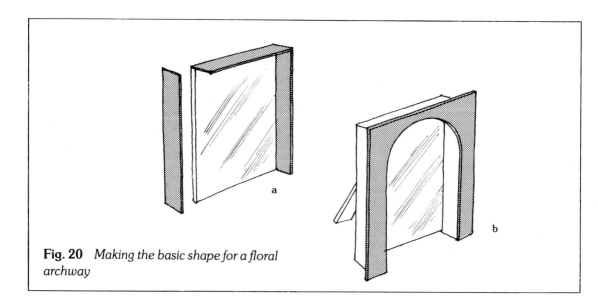

Fig. 20 *Making the basic shape for a floral archway*

Figurines as accessories

A figurine can very often provide inspiration for an arrangement, as it can either suggest the style of arrangement or the type of plant materials to be used. It may even be an indication and guide as to your choice of colour scheme. A figurine is an accessory when it is used in an arrangement but is not an integral part of the container. Inexpensive figurines which make ideal accessories can usually be found in the shops at Christmas time in the form of angels; Plates 9D and 10 illustrate examples. As these are often made from plastic it is quite easy to cut off their wings if you so desire. This was the case with the gilt figurine in Plate 9D and I found that when it was incorporated into the arrangement the marks easily became concealed, although a little paint would camouflage them if necessary. At other times, tiny china or plastic figurines can be found in gift shops.

MAKING ARCHWAYS

Archways are typical of an English country garden and for this reason I feel that a miniature replica creates a perfect setting for a miniature flower arrangement in which a small figure can be incorporated. The two archways illustrated in Plates 8D and 10 are both easy to make.

The archway in Plate 8D is made from coloured cardboard and is fitted to a small handbag mirror. To make this, measure the sides and across the top of the mirror and cut three pieces of cardboard of corresponding lengths and about 12 mm (½ in) in width. Stick these together and then attach them to the mirror to form a frame as shown in Fig. 20a. Cut another piece of cardboard 6 mm (¼ in) wider on each side and 6 mm (¼ in) higher than the frame. Draw and cut out an

38

arch shape as shown in Fig. 20b and stick this shape to the front of the frame. See page 51 for details of making a strut to enable the archway to stand. To decorate the archway, arrange and stick flowers and leaves in position using contact adhesive.

For the archway shown in Plate 10 I used two lengths of florists' silver wire, twisted together and bent into the shape of an arch. The ends are anchored into two knobs of floral clay, which are pressed firmly into position on a velvet-covered base edged with gold cord (see Fig. 21 for making bases). The floral clay also holds the tiny arrangements of plant materials which are linked to each other with placements of other plant materials stuck around the wire. A little figure (sold as a Christmas tree decoration) completes the scene.

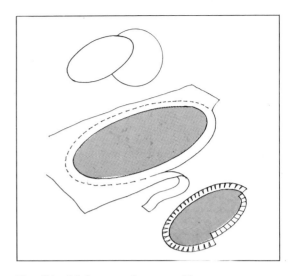

Fig. 21 *Making oval or round bases*

accentuate and highlight the main colouring of the plant materials. A greater impact of colour will be created in this way and visually the arrangement will appear more balanced.

BASES

If a base is used in a miniature flower arrangement it is important that it should have a purpose and relate to that arrangement. Size, shape, colour and texture are all vital factors to be carefully considered. Delightful arrangements can be created directly on to a base without the need for a container, which is particularly beneficial for the arranger who may have difficulty in finding suitable small items to use as containers. Alternatively, if carefully chosen, a base which supports a container can help to create balance, particularly with a pedestal-type container such as the one illustrated in Plate 6. The colouring of the base may also

MAKING BASES

Making your own bases is an ideal way to ensure that they are tailor-made to suit each individual arrangement. Because they are small they can be easily cut with scissors from a piece of card. Coloured card is adequate but plain white card covered with fabric makes a more attractive base. The fabric should be chosen for its suitability for both container and plant materials. Cut a piece of fabric 6 mm (¼ in) larger all round than the cardboard base. For oval or round bases cut out tiny notches in the fabric as shown in Fig. 21, but care should be taken to cut these less than 6 mm (¼ in) deep to prevent the finished base having a jagged edge. Position your fabric on the cardboard base, turn the notched edge over and stick down to the reverse side with glue. Cut a slightly smaller paper shape and stick this over the back to give the base a neat finish. On larger bases such as the one illustrated in Plate 10, a fine cord glued round the edge provides an attractive finish to an otherwise rather solid-looking base. If necessary the base can be raised with little feet in the form of beads glued to the underside.

NATURAL BASES

Natural bases – for example, wood, stone or slate – can be used either in their natural state or cut to a particular shape or size. I prefer the former. Bases such as these are particularly suitable to use for a simple arrangement of unsophisticated plant materials such as daisies or heather (see Plate 11). In many cases containers may be unnecessary as the arranger can create a more natural effect by making the arrangement directly on to the base. To hold the plant materials, tiny lumps of plasticine or floral clay can be pressed in position or, alternatively, small pieces of floral foam can be effectively glued.

moss to represent rocks, and little paste pots of water were carefully concealed to hold tiny bunches of fresh flowers. Even branches were poked into the moss to represent trees. It was the memory of this which inspired me to create the little scenes shown here. Each miniature landscape can be made directly on to a suitable base, which should be chosen for its colour, texture and type, depending on whatever scene is being depicted. Bases of natural material are on the whole more suited to this type of miniature work as they will form a more true representation of each individual landscape. Sometimes, however, it is necessary to use a base which although not authentic will nevertheless create the desired effect. The landscapes which I have illustrated show a variety of bases, each one carefully chosen to create the appropriate setting for the plant materials and accessories used. Landscapes such as these may not strictly be considered to be flower arrangements, but they are fun to create. They are also something which children with their small fingers find pleasure in making, and may well provide an introduction for them to the world of flower arranging.

CREATING MINIATURE LANDSCAPES

As a child I remember the fascination and sheer delight of making a moss garden on a plate. Tiny stones were placed between the

Plate 10 *An arrangement inspired by a Christmas angel*

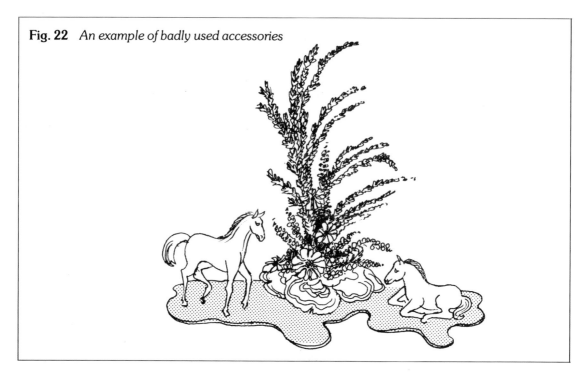

Fig. 22 *An example of badly used accessories*

ACCESSORIES FOR LANDSCAPE DESIGNS

For miniature landscape designs the most obvious choice of accessories are animals and birds. I find that the tiny creatures actually dictate the type of plant material that I use, and the type of scene that I create. It is for this reason that the landscapes illustrated differ so greatly from each other. Particularly suitable for this purpose are the miniature animals which are sold in toy shops, not only because they are the correct size but also because their surface texture is usually far more complementary to natural plant materials than that of the animals sold as ornaments. Apart from the unsuitable shiny surface of most china and glass ornaments, they usually lack the realistic lifelike poses of the toy shop animals, and it is of course this feature which is so necessary in an attempt to create a sense of movement within the arrangement. The chicks I used in Plate 11c are the mass-produced type which can be purchased around Easter time for cake decorations, etc.; but do remember to compare the features: some have the most marvellous expressions, while others can look most peculiar. Whenever accessories in the form of animals and birds are used in flower arrangements, restraint is necessary to avoid a cluttered look in which the accessories are dotted here and there (see Fig. 22), causing the eye to jump about rather than being led

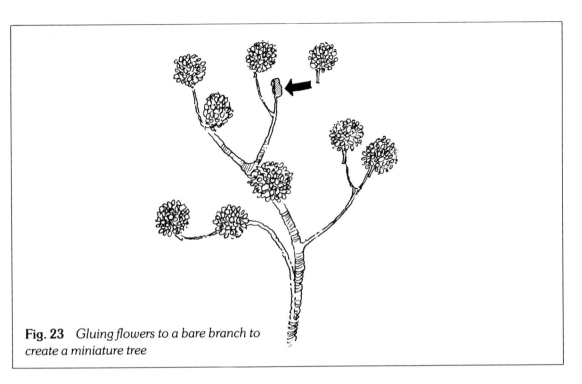

Fig. 23 *Gluing flowers to a bare branch to create a miniature tree*

uninterrupted through the arrangement, or where they actually dominate the plant materials. In miniature flower arranging this element of design is particularly important owing to the scale at which you are working. Miniature accessories are often difficult to find and I would always prefer to create an arrangement without an accessory rather than use something which in both size and type is not absolutely ideal.

MAKING MINIATURE TREES

Few natural landscapes are complete without trees, but when the fresh flower arranger creates a landscape design he or she is lim-ited to using branches of flowering shrubs or trees in season, or sprays of leaves that are easily accessible. The preserved flower arranger, and in particular the miniaturist, is able to create unique trees of exactly the right size, type and colour for virtually any chosen style of landscape design. From a selection of tiny preserved leaves, flowers, bare twigs or wispy pieces of tree root, creating miniature trees can be great fun (Fig. 23). As with all other ingredients of miniature arrangements, it is very important that the scale of each tree is correct, and although it should represent the tallest point of your landscape it should at the same time become an integral part of the design and not just tower above it as a solitary unit.

DISPLAYING MINIATURE ARRANGEMENTS

When it comes to displaying miniature arrangements this is really flower arranging with a difference for the arrangements created are semi-permanent. Many of my ideas illustrate types of arrangements which, if displayed in a suitable place in the home, can be interesting features of decoration just as any other form of miniatures would be. Carefully chosen positions in the home are absolutely essential if your miniature arrangements are to be seen at their best, and the most important consideration is that of scale. For example, it would be advisable not to position miniature arrangements haphazardly among large objects or to dot them around on furniture, particularly in close association with large fresh arrangements. Several miniature arrangements which are complementary to each other would make an interesting feature if grouped together on a small table where they could be viewed independently without fear of dominance or distraction. In such a grouping it is beneficial to have a theme, by which I mean something to link the group of arrangements together. It is possible to do this in many ways – through the choice of colour scheme, maybe, or with all the arrangements incorporating wood or stone. Another suggestion is to use a collection of brass or even silver items as containers, depending on which are most suited to the decor of the room. The choice made would automatically be reflected in the colour scheme of the plant materials.

Large arrangements are usually viewed from a distance, even if only from the other side of a room. Although we may take a closer look to observe a particular flower or seedhead, generally such arrangements are seen as an integral part of the surrounding decor. This is not so with miniature arrangements, however, for by their very nature they invite the viewer to look closely. This was borne out on one occasion I shall always remember, when I organized a flower festival entirely of preserved flowers. I placed some miniature arrangements on the top shelf of a tiered table and at the last minute decided to stage some extra miniatures on the lower shelf. During the three-day event I constantly observed what appeared to be prayer meetings around this table. This left me with little doubt that miniature arrangements should be designed to be looked at, but also, more important, to be looked into.

Plate 11 *Landscape designs incorporating miniature animals and birds*

44

A

B

C

D

PLAQUES, PICTURES AND VICTORIAN NOVELTIES

I feel that no book on the subject of minia-tures is complete without mentioning minia-ture pictures. I have a preference for using old frames but it is often necessary to collect these over a period of years. Readers who cannot easily find such frames should not despair. Photographic shops and studios now sell a wide range of miniature frames, many of which are quite inexpensive, and I have included details below for making re-cessed shapes which will enable the backs of frames to be extended to give adequate depth for miniature plant materials (see Plates 12 and 15c). Although miniature frames are delightful to look at and a pleas-ure to own, miniature plaques can be equal-ly attractive and desirable to make, involving little or no cost. Examples of some of my own ideas can be seen in Plate 13 and the details for making these are given on page 48. Influenced by the Victorian era, easily made and decorated novelties also create an effective use for preserved plant materials, and individually they make attractive and

interesting features if displayed in a suitable place (see page 44). Note, however, that although decorative, these are not technical-ly arrangements and before entering any of these in competitive classes for miniature flower arrangements it would be advisable to check with the schedule or even the orga-nizers.

RECESSED SHAPES FOR OVAL PICTURE FRAMES

If it is necessary to increase the depth of a picture frame in order for it to accommodate preserved flowers, you will need to make a recessed shape to fit behind the frame. To do this, measure round the inside of the rebate of the frame and cut a strip of cardboard (the pliable type which bends without cracking) the same length. The width of this strip will determine the depth of the recess and there-fore will vary according to the plant materials used. It must be wide enough to provide adequate clearance and prevent the plant

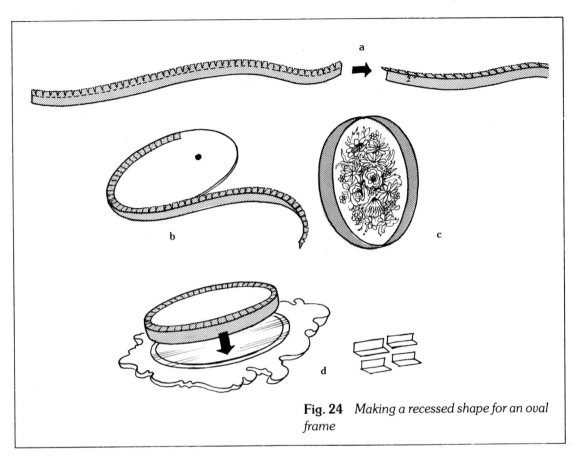

Fig. 24 *Making a recessed shape for an oval frame*

materials becoming squashed by the glass, plus an additional 6 mm (¼ in). Cut notches in the extra 6 mm (¼ in) as shown in Fig. 24a, and then bend this portion over and crease it. Cut an oval cardboard shape the same size as the rebate or picture area and glue the notched edge of the strip over this to form your box (see Fig. 24b).

If a suitable-coloured cardboard is used to make the box shape, the plant materials can be stuck directly on to this. However, if a fabric-lined box is preferred, cut two pieces of fabric: an oval piece to line the base, and a narrow piece to line the side. Using sharp scissors, make sure the fabric is cut along the grain and stick it to the cardboard immediately to avoid fraying. Use either a spray glue or, if this is not available, a thinly applied coat of latex adhesive, and apply the glue to the cardboard, not the fabric.

Make your arrangement of preserved plant materials (see Fig. 24c) and stick them in place using a quick-drying contact adhesive. If the frame is without a glass, get a piece cut to size and, after cleaning, position it in the rebate of the frame. Place the box shape behind the glass (see Fig. 24d) and secure it in place with tiny pieces of thin card folded in half and stuck to the side of the box and the back of the frame.

PLAQUES

I very seldom use square or oblong shapes for plaques as I feel these look more attractive when surrounded by a frame. Stiff cardboard, such as mounting board, is used to make the basic shapes for plaques; this can be purchased from most art shops and it is possible to buy off-cuts at very little cost from a picture framer. An alternative source of suitable cardboard is old cardboard boxes.

TRIPLE PLAQUE

To make this you will need: stiff cardboard, contact glue, a remnant of material, 460 mm (18 in) of 6 mm (¼ in) wide lace, and 305 mm (12 in) of 12 mm (½ in) wide ribbon. Cut three oval-shaped pieces of cardboard to the size shown in Fig. 25 and cover each one as described for bases on page 39. Cut the lace into three equal lengths, and glue each piece around the front edge of the three oval bases to form a pretty decorative border (see Fig. 25). Mark the position for attaching each one to the ribbon. The top and bottom ones should be 32 mm (1¼ in) from each end of

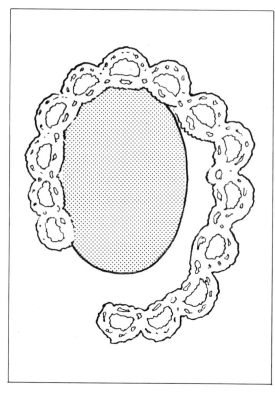

Fig. 25 *Making an oval shape for a triple plaque*

the ribbon, with the central one positioned an equal distance between the two. Stick these firmly in place. Almost all tiny flowers can be used for the arrangements, which should be confined to the area within the lace border. For the plaque in Plate 13 I chose colours to harmonize with the deep purple ribbon.

Plate 12 *Miniature picture, silver candlestick incorporating a birthday cake candle, and pewter box*

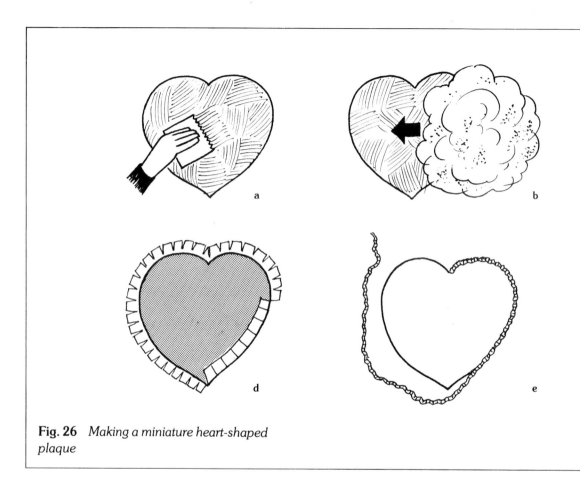

Fig. 26 *Making a miniature heart-shaped plaque*

MINIATURE HEART-SHAPED PLAQUE

I am quite sure that hearts and flowers go hand in hand as much today as they did in the days of our Victorian ancestors, so I thought it would be appropriate to design a miniature heart-shaped flower plaque (see Fig. 26) which could easily be used with other miniature Victorian novelties to form part of a display. To make this, cut a heart shape from a piece of thin cardboard. Smear glue over the surface on one side (a) and press on cotton wool or similar padding (b). Trim round the edge of the heart to cut away surplus padding. Then cut a piece of fabric about 12 mm (½ in) larger than the heart on all sides (c); cut 6 mm (¼ in) deep notches round the edge. Lay the fabric over the padding, turn the notched edge to the un-

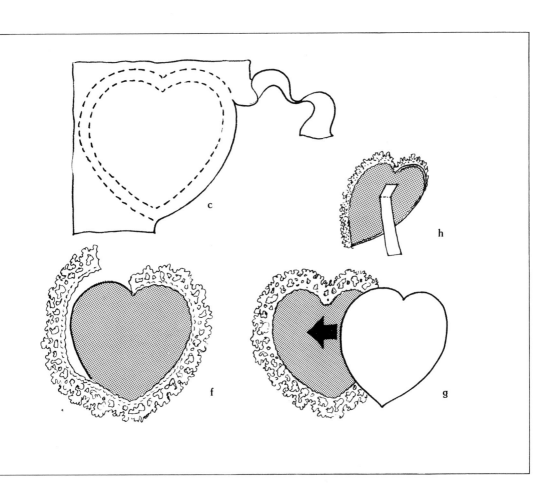

padded side and stick (d). Glue a narrow decorative cord round the edge (e). Run a gathering thread along one edge of some lace and pull up fairly tight to obtain a ruched effect. Stick the gathered edge to the edge of the plaque back (f). Cut a second heart shape from thin card and glue over the lace to neaten the back of the plaque (g). Make your arrangement on the front of the plaque and fix your plant materials with glue.

Making a stand

Individual plaques of any size can be made to stand by attaching a cardboard strut to the back. This is easy to do: Fig. 26h shows the shape to cut. The size will depend on the size of the plaque, of course. Score the cardboard across the dotted line, holding the plaque at the required angle, and stick the strut into a position which allows the plaque to stand at this angle.

Fig. 27 *Making a miniature posy*

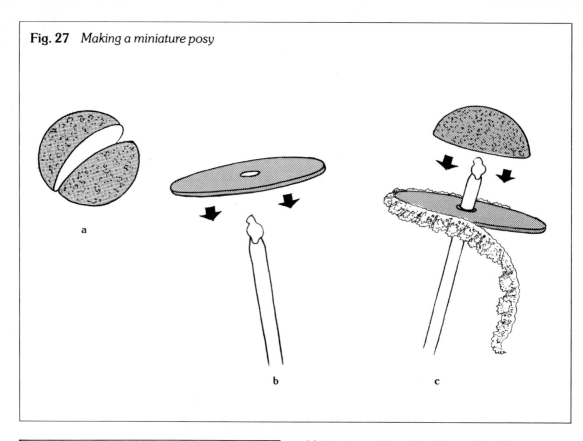

a

b

c

MINIATURE POSY

Reproducing a Victorian posy is by no means a new idea; it is something which appears to be equally popular with bridesmaids today as it was at the time of my own wedding, twenty-five years ago. Yet my idea of making a miniature posy is for a completely different reason. I felt that it would make a delightful gift, especially for an elderly lady, and would be particularly appropriate as an addition to a collection of Victorian nicknacks. To make the posy in Plate 13 you will need: half a small ball of plastic foam (Fig. 27a), a circle of cardboard slightly larger in diameter than the foam, 88 mm (3½ in) of dowelling or similar, 460 mm (18 in) each of lace and ribbon, and glue. Cut a small hole in the centre of the cardboard just large enough to take the dowelling. Put a blob of glue on one end of the dowelling and push it through the hole in the card-

Plate 13 *Triple plaque, heart-shaped plaque, and Victorian posy*

board and into the plastic foam (Fig. 27b). Gather the lace and glue it around the edge of the cardboard as shown in Fig. 27c. If you have only white lace available, why not dip it in coffee? I did! The coffee gives the lace the appearance of being antique, in keeping with the posy. Almost any tiny flowers can be used to create distinctive circles of colour around a slightly larger central flower. I have used a traditional red rose as my central flower, surrounded by a circle of yellow Statice. Next is a circle of flowers from the Double Pink Cherry, and the final circle is of purple/blue Statice. A small blob of glue on the tip of each tiny stem will secure the flowers firmly in place. Bind the dowelling with ribbon of a matching colour, allowing the two ends to hang as shown. You can vary the size of your posy if you wish; an even smaller one would also be attractive.

FLOWER ARRANGEMENT GREETINGS CARD

I am often asked how I get new ideas, and it is true to say that they are usually sparked off by something I have seen which I feel I can interpret in my own way using flowers. The elaborate greetings cards of the Victorian era have often been my inspiration, but the one in Plate 14 was inspired by a combination of Victorian cards and an 18 mm (¾ in) high sample perfume bottle, a hoarded treasure found in an old chest which I purchased

many years ago. Obviously not everyone will be able to find an identical bottle, so the measurements given for making this card should only be considered in relation to the tiny arrangement in the bottle. If you use an item which is larger or of a different shape, the card should be scaled accordingly. Alternative items for containers could include bottle tops, thimbles and empty seed-cases. You will need: stiff cardboard (the sort that will not crack when bent), thin pliable card (a postcard would be ideal), a remnant of thin fabric, a remnant of 12 mm (½ in) wide lace, and spray glue. Cut a piece of stiff cardboard 82 × 127 mm (3¼ × 5 in). Fold this in half, then mark and cut out an arched window in one half as shown in Fig. 28a. From the top of the cut-out piece of cardboard measure down 18 mm (¾ in) and cut across (Fig. 28b). Glue this piece of cardboard to the bottom of the window to form a shelf (Fig. 28c). Cover this and the front of the card with glue; position and carefully press down the fabric. Make sure that the glue covers the edges of the cardboard and that the fabric is well pressed down around the edge. Surplus fabric can now be cut away without fear of it fraying. Gather the lace and stick the gathered edge to the inside edge of the window (Fig. 28c). Finally, cut a piece of thin card 88 × 63 mm (3½ × 2½ in). Bend and stick this around the edge of the shelf and glue the side edges to the inside of the card. Fig. 28d shows the angle of the stuck card.

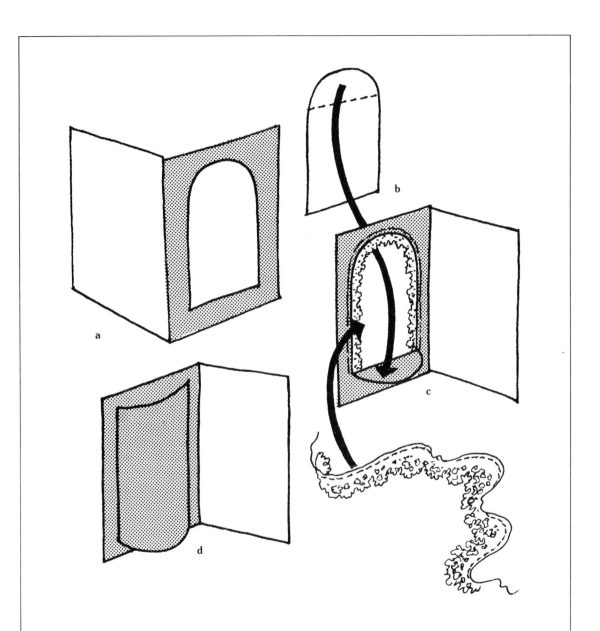

Fig. 28 *Making a flower arrangement greetings card*

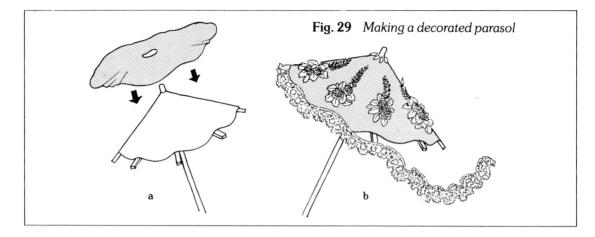

Fig. 29 *Making a decorated parasol*

a

b

PARASOL

I was sure that the parasol, being typically Victorian, should find a place in this chapter. But the difficulty in making an effective miniature parasol just to decorate with flowers made the project seem wildly impractical. I was just about to abandon the idea when I thought of the possible use of a cocktail umbrella as a base on which to work. These little umbrellas are inexpensive and easily obtainable, and I soon discovered that when covered and decorated with preserved flowers they make charming table gifts for guests at a party. I found it necessary to use an extremely lightweight fabric; for the parasol in Plate 14 I used silk shantung, a remnant from a friend's wedding dress material.

Details for covering

As such small scraps of fabric are needed there should be no real problem in finding suitable pieces; for example, discarded clothing (jumble sales are ideal places to ex-

plore), scraps left over from dressmaking, even obsolete samples from fabric shops. Turn the opened parasol upside down on to a piece of paper, cut a small hole and push the spike of the parasol through. Now draw round the edge to make a pattern which can be used to mark out and cut your own fabric covering. Lightly and evenly cover the outside of the parasol with glue; for very thin fabric a spray glue is most suitable. Now push the parasol spike through the hole in the fabric (see Fig. 29a), and press the two surfaces together. A narrow edging of 18 mm (¾ in) wide lace glued to the edge of the fabric neatens the raw edge and gives the parasol an attractive finish. You will be able to think of many ways of decorating your parasol. I chose to fix tiny arrangements of flowers with minute fronds of the Maidenhair Spleenwort fern to alternate sections, with a circle of tiny fern frond segments stuck round the spike (see Fig. 29b).

Plate 14 *Fan, flower arrangement greetings card, and parasol*

DECORATED FAN

Beautifully decorated fans have always won my admiration, and having decorated the parasol, the idea came to me of making a matching fan. I found that a great deal of experimenting was necessary to create a basic fan shape which was effective and yet easy to make. I had previously made a full-size fan with a balsa wood structure, but I soon discovered that for the inexperienced it would prove too difficult to cut the miniature shapes required. Eventually I decided that thin card would be adequate; in fact, even a postcard would be suitable.

Details of making the structure

Readers who, like myself, are not good at drawing may like to trace my husband's illustration (Fig. 30a). This gives the actual size of the ribs used for the fan in Plate 14. Mark and cut out eight identical ribs from the card. Then, using a large darning needle, pierce a hole through the rounded end of each rib as shown. Insert a pin, pushing it through all the holes. Cut the pin and secure the end at the back of the eighth rib with a blob of glue. This method of fixing actually enables the fan to be opened and closed.

Covering the fan

Open the structure and lay it on a piece of paper. Mark and cut out a shape 38 mm (1½ in) deep to fit across the top section of the fan as shown, allowing an extra 6 mm (¼ in) at each end to use as turnings. Cut a piece of fabric exactly the same size and glue the paper and fabric together (for details of the type of fabric and glue to use, see under 'Parasol'). While making sure that the ribs are evenly spaced, stick the paper side of the fabric-covered paper to them as shown, turning it over at each end and sticking it to the end ribs. With the back of the fan facing you, make a crease in the fabric-covered paper on the righthand side of each rib and also between each one, as shown in Fig. 30b, to enable the fan to be closed. Glue a strip of lace to the edge of the fan as shown in Fig. 30c. Tiny sprays of flowers can then be arranged and stuck in position between the ribs.

Although the measurements of some of my arrangements are given in the text, these should be regarded merely as a guide by those readers who are interested in creating arrangements only for their own homes or as gifts for friends: the same arrangements can be created larger or smaller as long as the size of the plant material in relation to container, accessory and base remains constant. However, those arrangers wishing to compete in the appropriate classes of shows or flower arrangement societies which are judged by NAFAS (National Association of Flower Arrangement Societies) rules should carefully observe the required measurements. The NAFAS definitions booklet divides small arrangements into two groups and specifies that a 'miniature design' must be not more than 102 mm (4 in) overall, and a 'petite design' must be more than 102 mm (4 in) and less than 229 mm (9 in) overall.

It has been my aim in this book to encourage the beginner and the more experienced

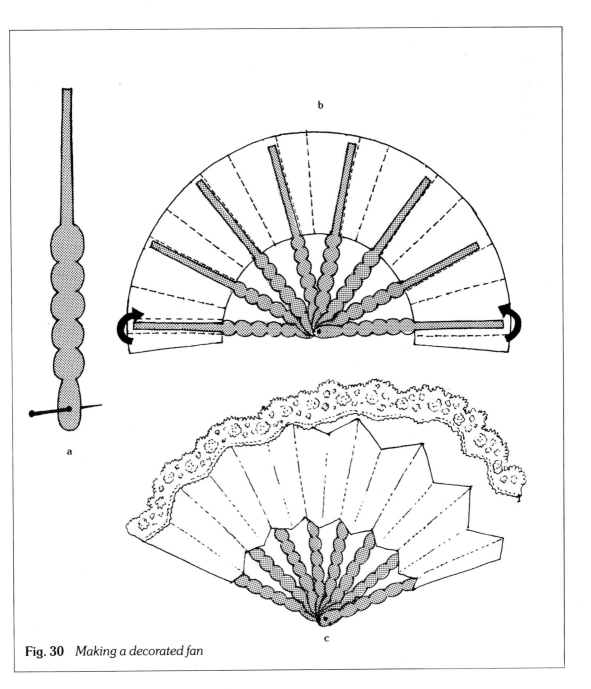

Fig. 30 *Making a decorated fan*

flower arranger alike to discover and explore the fascinating world of miniature preserved flower arranging. So, whether you intend to make arrangements to enter in competitions or just for fun, I hope that some of my ideas and designs will inspire you to create distinctive arrangements of your own. The results can be most attractive and will give much pleasure not only to the arranger but also to all those who see them.

OTHER BOOKS BY MAUREEN FOSTER

Preserved Flowers – Practical Methods and Creative Uses
Creating Pictures with Preserved Flowers
Flower Preserving for Beginners
Making Animal and Bird Collages with Grasses, Leaves, Seedheads and Cones
Creating Patterns from Grasses, Seedheads and Cones
The Art of Preserved Flower Arrangement

SUPPLIERS

Specially prepared flower preserving crystals can be obtained from M. F. Crystals (Dept B7), 77 Bulbridge Road, Wilton, Salisbury, Wiltshire SP2 0LE (send a stamped addressed envelope for details).

Flora Products, Stanley Gibbons Magazines Ltd, 5 Parkside, Christchurch Road, Ringwood, Hampshire BH24 3SH (send a stamped addressed envelope for details of products available).

Plate 15 *Arrangements of gold-painted plant materials in gilt-coloured containers*

A

B

C

61